LITTLE HISTORIES

Aztec Times

Anita Ganeri

Kingfisher

Contents

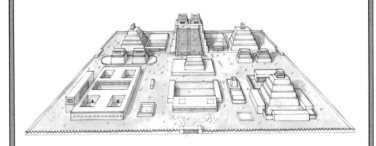

A warlike people

The Aztecs were a wandering tribe who lived in the country we now call Mexico. About 600 years ago, these fierce, warlike people settled down and built a village. Within 100 years the Aztecs ruled over a large empire, and the village had become a splendid city called Tenochtitlan. In the middle of the city, the Aztecs built enormous, pyramid-shaped temples to their gods.

The Aztec Empire

At the height of its power in the early 1500s, the Aztec Empire stretched all the way across Mexico. It contained nearly 500 towns and over 15 million

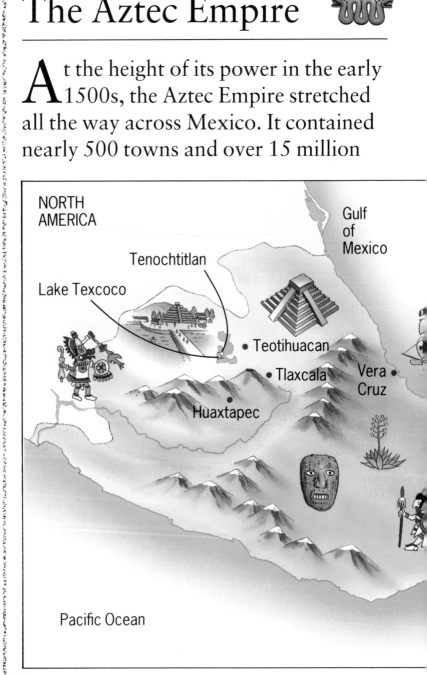

NORTH AMERICA

Gulf of Mexico

Tenochtitlan

Lake Texcoco

Teotihuacan

Tlaxcala

Vera Cruz

Huaxtapec

Pacific Ocean

people, most of whom belonged to other tribes. But Aztec rule came to a sudden end in 1521, when Spanish invaders, greedy for the Aztecs' wealth, captured Tenochtitlan and destroyed the empire.

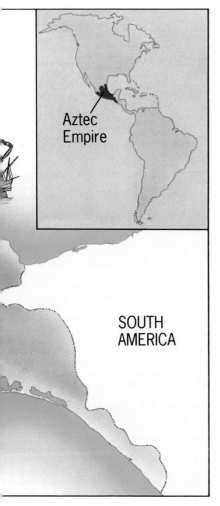

Aztec Empire

SOUTH AMERICA

When the Spanish soldier Hernando Cortés and his men arrived in Tenochtitlan in 1519, they were amazed by its size and splendour. They were determined to steal the Aztecs' gold, and the many other precious objects they saw.

City in the swamp

Tenochtitlan began as a small village in the middle of the swampy Lake Texcoco. The Aztecs were brilliant engineers, and they built roads to link the island to the mainland. Canals threaded through the city, and people travelled about in canoes. Aqueducts brought fresh water to the town.

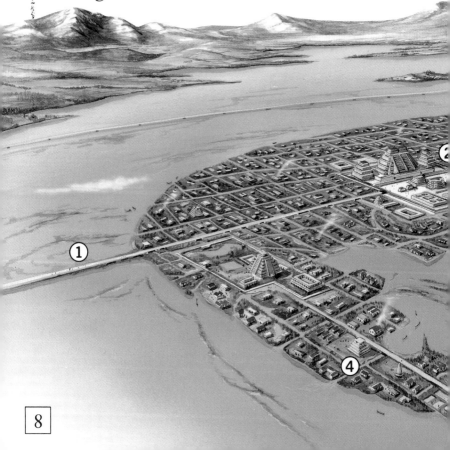

A SIGN FROM THE GODS

According to legend, the Aztecs settled at the spot where they saw an eagle perched on a prickly cactus. They had been told to look out for this sign by one of their gods.

KEY TO CITY

① Causeway, a road to the city
② Temple area
③ Covered aqueduct
④ Canal

③

The emperor

The ruler of the Aztecs was the emperor. He was treated like a god, and could only be spoken to by high priests and nobles. On special occasions, he was carried through the city on a splendid throne. Ordinary people were not allowed to look at him, but kept their eyes on the ground.

Much of the emperor's wealth came from the towns and people conquered by his army. Defeated tribes had to make payments, called tribute, to the Aztec Empire.

The Aztecs didn't have money, so this tribute was paid with valuables such as gold, precious stones, clothing, exotic feathers, spears and other weapons.

The emperor ruled from a magnificent palace, near the Great Temple. It was so large that you could walk all day without seeing all of it!

Temple of death

The Great Temple lay at the very heart of Tenochtitlan. During special festivals, thousands of people were led up the steps of the temple shrines to be killed, as a gift to the gods. Many of the victims were prisoners of war.

Keeping the gods happy was very important to the Aztecs. They believed that the gods brought the rain that made their crops grow, and gave victory to their armies in battle.

AZTEC GODS

Huitzilopochtli, god of war.
Tlaloc, god of rain and crops.
Quetzalcoatl, god of the wind and learning.

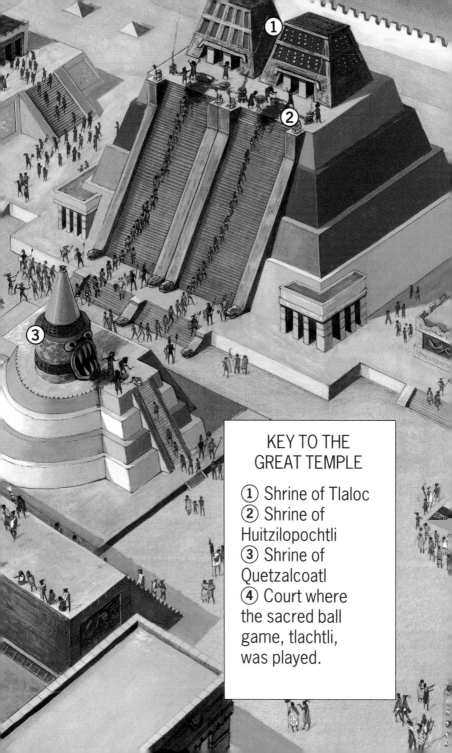

KEY TO THE
GREAT TEMPLE

① Shrine of Tlaloc
② Shrine of
Huitzilopochtli
③ Shrine of
Quetzalcoatl
④ Court where
the sacred ball
game, tlachtli,
was played.

The sacred game

In Aztec times, sport and games were an important part of religious ceremonies. There was even a special stone court for the sacred game of tlachtli in the Great Temple. Only noblemen were allowed to play, and the stakes were high – the losers lost all their possessions to the winners, and were often sacrificed to the gods!

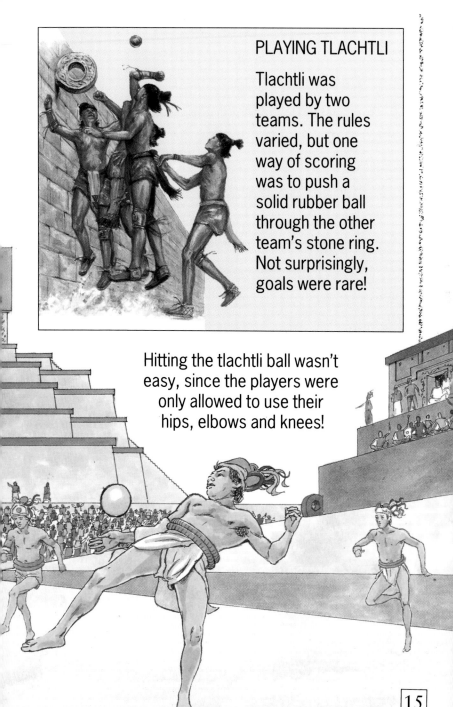

PLAYING TLACHTLI

Tlachtli was played by two teams. The rules varied, but one way of scoring was to push a solid rubber ball through the other team's stone ring. Not surprisingly, goals were rare!

Hitting the tlachtli ball wasn't easy, since the players were only allowed to use their hips, elbows and knees!

15

Training for war

All ordinary Aztec boys knew that one day they would have to go to war. They were sent to schools called telpochcalli, where they were taught to handle weapons and fight bravely.

When a young man had taken three prisoners in battle, he became a full warrior. He was then allowed to tie his hair in a topknot, and wear a headdress.

◁ Some of the best warriors were called the Jaguars, and wore fur skins and fur helmets. Another group was the Eagles, who wore feathered suits and helmets.

▷ Aztec warriors fought with spears, bows and arrows, and wooden clubs edged with sharp pieces of stone.

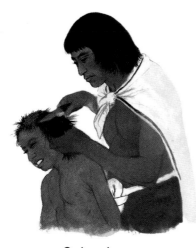

△ School was very strict. This young boy is having his head shaved for failing a test.

MAKE A SHIELD

You will need card, a pencil, some scraps of cloth, scissors and glue.

1 Cut an oval shape from the card. Draw on a simple design in pencil.

2 Cut the cloth into shapes that fit the design, and glue to the shield.

3 Cut a strip of card for a handle, and glue this to the back of the shield.

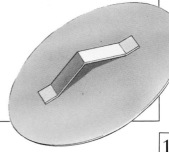

Clothing

Aztecs could tell how important people were by the way they were dressed. Nobles wore fine cotton clothes and feather headdresses, but ordinary people just had simple clothes made from cactus fibre. There were strict rules about jewellery, too. Only the emperor and his nobles could wear precious turquoises.

Men wore loin cloths, and cloaks knotted at the shoulder.

Women wore wrap-around skirts and short-sleeved blouses. Married women had to coil their hair up on top of their heads.

This headdress once belonged to an Aztec ruler. It was made of bright green feathers, from the tropical quetzal bird.

MAKE A ROYAL HEADDRESS

You'll need some thin card, glue, scissors, poster paints and a stapler.

1 Cut out these two identical shapes from card. Bend one of them into a circle, and check that it fits around your head.

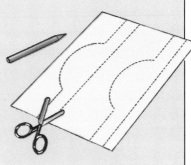

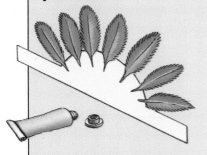

2 Cut some feather shapes from card, and glue the ends to one head piece.

3 Spread glue on the second head piece, and press both pieces together. Paint the front, and staple the ends together.

Farming the swamp

The Aztecs farmed plots of land called chinampas. These were built on the lake, from layers of reeds and leaves, covered with rich black mud. Wooden posts and willow trees were placed around each plot, to hold it together. The farmers also fished and hunted birds on the lake.

Cacao tree

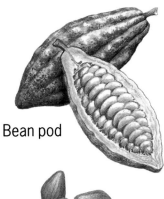

Bean pod

Cacao beans

Beans from the wild cacao tree were very valuable to the Aztecs, and were often used just like money. Thieves sometimes made fake cacao beans out of wax!

Rich people crushed the beans, to make a spicy chocolate drink.

A SPICY DRINK

You'll need:
125 g chocolate;
1 mugful milk;
1 drop vanilla essence; $\frac{1}{2}$ tsp ground cinnamon

1 Grate the chocolate.
2 Ask an adult to heat the milk in a saucepan.

3 Pour the hot milk into a mug, and stir in the chocolate.
4 Add the vanilla essence and the cinnamon. Stir well.

21

See inside a home

Ordinary Aztec people lived in small mud huts with thatched roofs. They had very little furniture, and the family slept on reed mats on the hard earth floor. For cooking, every home had a fire with a round, clay slab, called a comal.

The main food was maize. It was ground into flour, which was used to make pancakes called tortillas. These were baked on the comal, and eaten with spicy beans and tomatoes. This food is still popular in Mexico today.

Women spun yarn, and wove it to make the family's clothing and blankets. One end of the weaving loom was attached to the weaver by a belt.

KEY TO HOUSE

① Comal
② Stone for grinding maize into flour
③ Spindles for weaving
④ Blankets and clay pots, for market

Market day

Thousands of people visited the markets in Tenochtitlan, where merchants sold fruit, vegetables, clay pots, cloth, skins, precious stones and tropical feathers. Market inspectors made sure that traders charged a fair price, and that no-one was cheated!

The market was not just for buying goods. It was also a place where people could chat with their friends, and catch up on all the latest news.

MARKET FARE

Avocados, tomatoes and tangy limes were some of the produce on sale at an Aztec market.

Avocado

Tomato

Lime

Merchant spies

The exotic market goods were
brought to Tenochtitlan by
merchants, called pochteca. Their
trading expeditions took them over
high, snow-covered mountains to the
most distant parts of the empire.

They went north to find precious
turquoises, and to the hot lowlands for
cacao beans and bright parrot feathers.

Some merchants also acted as spies
for the emperor. Their job was to bring
back information about any towns or
cities that seemed to be growing too
rich or powerful.

Keeping records

The Aztecs used a writing system made up of small pictures which stood for ideas and sounds. Each of the pictures was drawn on paper made from fig tree bark. Long books were made by joining pieces of paper into a strip, and folding them up. Some books were about Aztec history and religion, while others were used to record tributes paid to the empire.

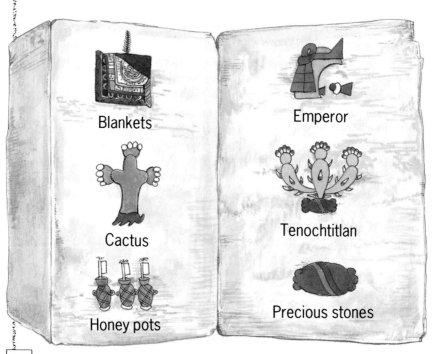

Blankets

Emperor

Cactus

Tenochtitlan

Honey pots

Precious stones

The Aztecs invented their own calendars. This Aztec sun stone shows the Sun god in the centre, with the signs of the Aztec days around it.

AN AZTEC SUN STONE

First, you will need to mix $1\frac{1}{2}$ cups of plain flour with 1 cup of salt. Add $1\frac{1}{2}$ cups of water, and mix to form a soft dough.

1 Roll out the dough. Cut into a circle, using a plate as a guide.
2 Using smaller plates, mark more circles in the middle.

3 Draw symbols in the dough, then bake for about $\frac{3}{4}$ hour at gas mark 2/170° C.

Glossary

aqueduct – a covered canel built to carry water

cacao – a tree whose seeds, or beans, are used to make cocoa powder for drinks and chocolate

calendar – a way to split up the year into months, weeks and days

conquer – another word for defeat

empire – a large area of land ruled by an emperor

engineer – someone who designs and builds things, such as roads and bridges

expedition – a journey in search of something

invader – someone who attacks and takes control of someone else's land

loincloth – a piece of cloth worn wrapped around the hips and bottom

maize – a crop that is also called corn, for example corn on the cob

pyramid – a large, stone building with sloping sides, where sacrifices were made to the gods

shrine – a holy place

tribute – a payment made by a people to their emperor

turquoise – a blue or pale-green gemstone